45 Valentine's Day Recipes for Home

By: Kelly Johnson

Table of Contents

Appetizers:

- Caprese Skewers with Heart-Shaped Mozzarella
- Smoked Salmon Rose Canapés
- Heart-Shaped Bruschetta
- Cranberry Brie Bites

Main Courses:

- Filet Mignon with Red Wine Reduction
- Lobster Tail with Garlic Butter
- Chicken Alfredo Pasta with Heart-Shaped Vegetables
- Vegetarian-Stuffed Bell Peppers

Sides:

- Roasted Asparagus Bundles
- Heart-Shaped Garlic Bread
- Parmesan Roasted Brussels Sprouts

Desserts:

- Chocolate Covered Strawberries
- Red Velvet Cupcakes
- Molten Lava Cakes
- Raspberry Chocolate Mousse
- Heart-Shaped Linzer Cookies

Drinks:

- Raspberry Champagne Cocktail
- Strawberry Mint Lemonade
- Chocolate Martini

Breakfast/Brunch:

- Heart-Shaped Pancakes
- Eggs Benedict with Heart-Shaped Toast
- Red Velvet Waffles

Extras:

- Heart-Shaped Fruit Salad
- Love Potion No. 9 Smoothie

Cocktails:

- Pomegranate Martini
- Rose Sangria
- Champagne Jello Shots

Romantic Dinners for Two:

- Baked Salmon with Lemon-Dill sauce
- Shrimp Scampi
- Couples Cooking Class Pizza

Sweets and Treats:

- Valentine's Day Truffles
- Heart-Shaped Red Velvet Whoopie Pies
- Cherry Chocolate Cheesecake

Cute and Playful:

- Love Bug Cupcakes
- Heart-Shaped Rice Krispie Treats
- Chocolate Covered Pretzel Rods

Special Breakfast in Bed:

- Heart-Shaped Breakfast Burritos
- Berry Parfait
- Heart-Shaped Avocado Toast

Intimate Dinners:

- Steak and Shrimp Surf and Turf
- Pasta in Pink Vodka Sauce
- Vegetarian Heart-Stuffed Bell Peppers

Appetizers:

Caprese Skewers with Heart-Shaped Mozzarella

Ingredients:

- Fresh mozzarella cheese (preferably in a ball or log shape)
- Cherry tomatoes
- Fresh basil leaves
- Balsamic glaze
- Olive oil
- Salt and pepper to taste
- Heart-shaped cookie cutter
- Wooden skewers

Instructions:

Prepare Mozzarella Hearts:
- Slice the fresh mozzarella into rounds. Using a heart-shaped cookie cutter, cut out heart shapes from the mozzarella slices. If you can't find a heart-shaped cookie cutter, you can carefully shape the mozzarella into hearts using a knife.

Assemble Skewers:
- Thread a cherry tomato onto the wooden skewer, followed by a basil leaf, and then a heart-shaped mozzarella piece. Repeat the pattern until the skewer is filled.

Arrange on Platter:
- Arrange the Caprese skewers on a serving platter or plate.

Drizzle with Balsamic Glaze:
- In a small bowl, mix balsamic glaze with a bit of olive oil. Drizzle the balsamic glaze over the skewers for added flavor. Alternatively, you can also serve the glaze on the side for dipping.

Season and Serve:
- Sprinkle the skewers with a pinch of salt and pepper to taste. This step is optional, as the mozzarella and balsamic glaze already provide plenty of flavor.

Chill (Optional):
- If you prefer, you can refrigerate the Caprese skewers for a short time before serving, especially if you want them to be cool and refreshing.

Serve and Enjoy:
- Serve the Caprese Skewers immediately, and enjoy this elegant and tasty appetizer with your loved ones.

Tips:

- Fresh Ingredients: Use the freshest mozzarella, cherry tomatoes, and basil leaves for the best flavor.
- Balsamic Glaze: You can find balsamic glaze in most grocery stores, or you can make your own by reducing balsamic vinegar on the stove until it thickens.

These Caprese Skewers with Heart-Shaped Mozzarella are not only delicious but also add a romantic touch to your appetizer spread. They're perfect for celebrating special moments with someone you love. Enjoy!

Smoked Salmon Rose Canapés

Ingredients:

- Smoked salmon slices
- Cream cheese, softened
- Fresh chives or dill, finely chopped
- Lemon zest
- Black pepper
- Baguette or crackers

Instructions:

Prepare Cream Cheese Mixture:
- In a bowl, mix the softened cream cheese with finely chopped chives or dill. Add a bit of freshly grated lemon zest for a burst of freshness. Season with black pepper to taste. Mix well until all the ingredients are combined.

Shape Salmon Roses:
- Take a slice of smoked salmon and lay it flat. Place a small amount of the cream cheese mixture at one end of the salmon slice. Carefully roll the salmon, starting from the cream cheese end, to form a rose shape. Repeat until you have the desired number of salmon roses.

Chill (Optional):
- If time allows, you can refrigerate the smoked salmon roses for a short time to firm them up slightly. This step is optional but can make them easier to handle.

Prepare Bread or Crackers:
- Slice the baguette into thin rounds or use your favorite crackers as the base for the canapés.

Assemble Canapés:
- Place a small dollop of the cream cheese mixture onto each baguette round or cracker. Gently press a smoked salmon rose on top of the cream cheese, securing it in place.

Garnish (Optional):
- Garnish the canapés with additional chopped chives, dill, or a sprinkle of lemon zest for a decorative touch.

Serve and Enjoy:
- Arrange the Smoked Salmon Rose Canapés on a serving platter and serve immediately.

Tips:

- Quality Smoked Salmon: Choose high-quality smoked salmon for the best flavor and texture.
- Variations: Experiment with different herbs and seasonings in the cream cheese mixture, such as adding a hint of horseradish or capers for extra depth of flavor.

These Smoked Salmon Rose Canapés are not only visually stunning but also a delightful combination of creamy and savory flavors. They are sure to impress your guests at any special gathering or celebration. Enjoy!

Heart-Shaped Bruschetta

Ingredients:

- Baguette or Italian bread
- Ripe tomatoes, diced
- Fresh basil leaves, chopped
- Garlic cloves, peeled
- Extra-virgin olive oil
- Balsamic glaze (optional)
- Salt and pepper to taste

Instructions:

Preheat Oven:
- Preheat your oven to 375°F (190°C).

Slice the Bread:
- Cut the baguette or Italian bread into slices, approximately 1/2 inch thick.

Cut Heart Shapes:
- Using a heart-shaped cookie cutter or a knife, cut heart shapes out of each bread slice. Place the heart-shaped bread pieces on a baking sheet.

Toast the Bread:
- Toast the heart-shaped bread in the preheated oven for about 5-7 minutes or until the edges are golden brown. Keep an eye on them to prevent burning.

Prepare Bruschetta Topping:
- In a bowl, combine diced tomatoes and chopped fresh basil. Drizzle with olive oil and season with salt and pepper. Toss the mixture until well combined.

Rub with Garlic:
- Take a peeled garlic clove and rub it over the toasted side of each heart-shaped bread. This imparts a subtle garlic flavor.

Top with Bruschetta Mixture:
- Spoon the tomato and basil mixture onto the center of each heart-shaped bread, ensuring an even distribution of toppings.

Optional Balsamic Glaze:
- If desired, drizzle a small amount of balsamic glaze over each heart-shaped bruschetta for added sweetness and visual appeal.

Serve and Enjoy:

- Arrange the heart-shaped bruschetta on a serving platter and serve immediately.

Tips:

- Fresh Ingredients: Use ripe and flavorful tomatoes, as well as fresh basil, for the best taste.
- Customize Toppings: Feel free to add other ingredients to the tomato and basil mixture, such as minced garlic, red onion, or mozzarella cheese.

This heart-shaped bruschetta is a charming appetizer that adds a touch of romance to your meal. Whether it's a special date night or a celebration, these delightful bites are sure to impress. Enjoy!

Cranberry Brie Bites

Ingredients:

- 1 sheet of puff pastry, thawed
- Brie cheese, cut into small cubes
- Cranberry sauce (homemade or store-bought)
- Fresh rosemary sprigs (for garnish, optional)
- 1 egg (beaten, for egg wash)

Instructions:

Preheat Oven:
- Preheat your oven to 375°F (190°C).

Prepare Puff Pastry:
- On a lightly floured surface, roll out the puff pastry sheet. If it's not already in a square or rectangle shape, you can gently shape it.

Cut Puff Pastry:
- Cut the puff pastry into small squares, large enough to wrap around a cube of Brie.

Place Brie and Cranberry:
- Place a small cube of Brie in the center of each puff pastry square. Top the Brie with a small dollop of cranberry sauce.

Fold and Seal:
- Carefully fold the corners of the puff pastry over the Brie and cranberry, creating a little package. Pinch the edges to seal.

Brush with Egg Wash:
- Brush the tops of the puff pastry with beaten egg. This will give them a golden-brown finish when baked.

Bake:
- Place the Cranberry Brie Bites on a baking sheet lined with parchment paper. Bake in the preheated oven for about 12-15 minutes or until the puff pastry is golden and puffed.

Garnish (Optional):
- Once out of the oven, garnish each bite with a small sprig of fresh rosemary if desired.

Serve and Enjoy:
- Allow the Cranberry Brie Bites to cool for a few minutes before serving. They can be enjoyed warm.

Tips:

- Brie Size: Adjust the size of the Brie cubes and the amount of cranberry sauce based on your preferences.
- Make-Ahead: You can assemble the Cranberry Brie Bites ahead of time and refrigerate until you're ready to bake them.

These Cranberry Brie Bites are perfect for holiday gatherings, cocktail parties, or any occasion where you want to impress your guests with a delicious and elegant appetizer. Enjoy!

Main Courses:

Filet Mignon with Red Wine Reduction

Ingredients:

- 2 filet mignon steaks (6-8 ounces each), at room temperature
- Salt and black pepper, to taste
- 1 tablespoon olive oil
- 2 tablespoons unsalted butter

For the Red Wine Reduction:

- 1 cup red wine (choose a good-quality red wine)
- 1/2 cup beef broth
- 1 shallot, finely chopped
- 1 tablespoon balsamic vinegar
- 1 teaspoon Dijon mustard
- Salt and black pepper, to taste

Instructions:

Preheat Oven:
- Preheat your oven to 400°F (200°C).

Season the Steaks:
- Pat the filet mignon steaks dry with a paper towel. Season both sides generously with salt and black pepper.

Sear the Steaks:
- In an oven-safe skillet, heat the olive oil over medium-high heat. Add the steaks and sear on each side for about 2-3 minutes or until they develop a nice brown crust.

Finish in the Oven:
- Transfer the skillet to the preheated oven and roast the filet mignon for about 5-7 minutes for medium-rare, or longer if you prefer your steak more well-done. Adjust the time based on your desired doneness.

Rest the Steaks:
- Remove the steaks from the oven and let them rest on a plate, tented with foil, for about 5-10 minutes. This allows the juices to redistribute.

Prepare Red Wine Reduction:

- While the steaks are resting, prepare the red wine reduction. In the same skillet over medium heat, add chopped shallot and sauté until softened.

Add Wine and Broth:
- Pour in the red wine, beef broth, balsamic vinegar, and Dijon mustard. Stir to combine. Allow the mixture to simmer and reduce by half.

Season and Finish Sauce:
- Season the sauce with salt and black pepper to taste. Stir in the butter, allowing it to melt and thicken the sauce.

Serve:
- Plate the rested filet mignon steaks and drizzle the red wine reduction sauce over them.

Garnish (Optional):
- Garnish with fresh herbs like thyme or rosemary if desired.

Enjoy:
- Serve the Filet Mignon with Red Wine Reduction immediately and enjoy this restaurant-quality dish at home.

Tips:

- Temperature Check: For the perfect doneness, use a meat thermometer to check the internal temperature. Aim for 130°F (54°C) for medium-rare, 140°F (60°C) for medium, and so on.
- Wine Choice: Use a red wine that you enjoy drinking since its flavor will greatly influence the sauce.

This Filet Mignon with Red Wine Reduction is a decadent and flavorful dish that's sure to impress your guests or loved ones. Enjoy the rich and savory experience!

Lobster Tail with Garlic Butter

Ingredients:

- 2 lobster tails (6-8 ounces each)
- Salt and black pepper, to taste
- 1/2 cup unsalted butter, melted
- 4 cloves garlic, minced
- 1 tablespoon fresh parsley, chopped
- Lemon wedges, for serving

Instructions:

Preheat Oven:
- Preheat your oven to 375°F (190°C).

Prepare Lobster Tails:
- Use kitchen shears to cut through the top of the lobster shells lengthwise, stopping at the tail. Gently pull the shell apart to expose the lobster meat, leaving it attached at the base.

Season Lobster Tails:
- Season the lobster meat with salt and black pepper to taste. Place the lobster tails on a baking sheet or in an oven-safe dish.

Garlic Butter Mixture:
- In a small bowl, mix melted butter, minced garlic, and chopped parsley to create the garlic butter mixture.

Brush with Garlic Butter:
- Brush the lobster meat generously with the garlic butter mixture, making sure to get the butter into the cuts you made in the shells.

Bake:
- Bake the lobster tails in the preheated oven for about 12-15 minutes or until the lobster meat is opaque and cooked through. The shells will turn bright red when done.

Baste (Optional):
- While baking, baste the lobster tails with additional garlic butter every 5 minutes for extra flavor and moisture.

Serve:
- Remove the lobster tails from the oven and serve immediately. Garnish with additional chopped parsley if desired.

Serve with Lemon Wedges:

- Serve the lobster tails with lemon wedges on the side for a fresh citrusy touch.

Tips:

- Lobster Tail Size: Adjust the cooking time based on the size of the lobster tails. Larger tails may require a few extra minutes in the oven.
- Broiling Option: If you prefer, you can broil the lobster tails for the last couple of minutes to get a slightly charred and caramelized finish on the garlic butter.

This Lobster Tail with Garlic Butter recipe is a delightful way to showcase the natural sweetness of lobster. Enjoy the rich, succulent meat dipped in the flavorful garlic butter for a truly indulgent dining experience.

Chicken Alfredo Pasta with Heart-Shaped Vegetables

Ingredients:

- 8 ounces fettuccine or your favorite pasta
- 2 boneless, skinless chicken breasts
- Salt and black pepper, to taste
- 2 tablespoons olive oil
- 3 cloves garlic, minced
- 1 cup heavy cream
- 1 cup grated Parmesan cheese
- 1/2 cup unsalted butter
- 1 cup broccoli florets, blanched
- 1 cup cherry tomatoes, halved
- Fresh basil leaves, for garnish
- Parmesan shavings, for garnish (optional)

Instructions:

Cook Pasta:
- Cook the fettuccine or pasta according to the package instructions until al dente. Drain and set aside.

Prepare Chicken:
- Season the chicken breasts with salt and black pepper. In a skillet over medium-high heat, add olive oil. Cook the chicken breasts until golden brown on each side and cooked through. Remove from the skillet and let them rest for a few minutes before slicing into thin strips.

Make Alfredo Sauce:
- In the same skillet, add minced garlic and sauté for about 1 minute until fragrant. Lower the heat to medium, then add the heavy cream, grated Parmesan cheese, and butter. Stir continuously until the cheese is melted, and the sauce is smooth.

Add Vegetables:
- Toss in the blanched broccoli florets and halved cherry tomatoes into the Alfredo sauce. Stir until the vegetables are coated with the sauce and heated through.

Combine Pasta and Chicken:
- Add the cooked fettuccine to the skillet, tossing it with the Alfredo sauce and vegetables until well coated. Add the sliced chicken on top.

Shape Vegetables into Hearts:

- Using a heart-shaped cookie cutter or a knife, cut heart shapes out of the broccoli florets and cherry tomato halves. This adds a romantic touch to the dish.

Serve:
- Plate the Chicken Alfredo Pasta, arranging the heart-shaped vegetables on top. Garnish with fresh basil leaves and Parmesan shavings if desired.

Enjoy:
- Serve immediately and enjoy this heartwarming and delicious Chicken Alfredo Pasta.

Tips:

- Fresh Herbs: Consider adding fresh herbs like basil or parsley for added flavor and a burst of color.
- Vegetable Substitutions: Feel free to include other heart-shaped vegetables like bell peppers or zucchini.

This Chicken Alfredo Pasta with Heart-Shaped Vegetables is not only a feast for the taste buds but also a visual delight, making it a perfect dish for a romantic dinner or any special celebration. Enjoy the love-filled meal!

Vegetarian-Stuffed Bell Peppers

Ingredients:

- 4 large bell peppers, any color
- 1 cup quinoa, cooked
- 1 can (15 oz) black beans, drained and rinsed
- 1 cup corn kernels (fresh, frozen, or canned)
- 1 cup cherry tomatoes, diced
- 1 cup shredded cheese (cheddar, Monterey Jack, or your choice)
- 1 teaspoon ground cumin
- 1 teaspoon chili powder
- 1/2 teaspoon garlic powder
- Salt and black pepper, to taste
- 1/2 cup fresh cilantro, chopped
- 1 cup tomato sauce or salsa (for topping)
- Optional toppings: Avocado slices, sour cream, chopped green onions

Instructions:

Preheat Oven:
- Preheat your oven to 375°F (190°C).

Prepare Bell Peppers:
- Cut the tops off the bell peppers, remove seeds, and any membranes. If needed, slice a small portion off the bottom to help them stand upright. Lightly brush the outside of the peppers with olive oil and place them in a baking dish.

Prepare Filling:
- In a large bowl, combine cooked quinoa, black beans, corn, cherry tomatoes, shredded cheese, ground cumin, chili powder, garlic powder, salt, black pepper, and chopped cilantro. Mix well until all ingredients are evenly distributed.

Stuff Peppers:
- Stuff each bell pepper with the quinoa and vegetable mixture, pressing it down gently to pack it in.

Top with Tomato Sauce:
- Spoon tomato sauce or salsa over the top of each stuffed pepper.

Bake:
- Cover the baking dish with aluminum foil and bake in the preheated oven for 25-30 minutes or until the peppers are tender.

Optional Cheese Topping:
- If you like, remove the foil, sprinkle a bit more cheese on top of each stuffed pepper, and bake for an additional 5-7 minutes or until the cheese is melted and bubbly.

Serve:
- Remove from the oven, let them cool slightly, and serve the Vegetarian Stuffed Bell Peppers with optional toppings like avocado slices, sour cream, or chopped green onions.

Tips:

- Customize Fillings: Feel free to customize the filling with other vegetables like diced zucchini, spinach, or mushrooms.
- Spice Level: Adjust the spices and seasonings to suit your taste preferences.

These Vegetarian Stuffed Bell Peppers are not only delicious but also a colorful and wholesome meal. They're a perfect option for a meatless dinner or a crowd-pleasing dish for guests with various dietary preferences. Enjoy!

Sides:

Roasted Asparagus Bundles

Ingredients:

- Fresh asparagus spears (1 bunch)
- Olive oil
- Salt and black pepper, to taste
- Garlic cloves, minced (optional)
- Lemon zest (optional)
- Parmesan cheese, grated (optional)

Instructions:

Preheat Oven:
- Preheat your oven to 400°F (200°C).

Prepare Asparagus:
- Wash the asparagus spears and trim the tough ends. If the asparagus is thick, you can peel the lower part for a more tender result.

Bundle Asparagus:
- Group 5-6 asparagus spears together to form a bundle. Tie the bundle together with kitchen twine or secure with a piece of thin asparagus spear.

Season Asparagus:
- Place the asparagus bundles on a baking sheet. Drizzle with olive oil, ensuring the bundles are well-coated. Season with salt and black pepper to taste. Add minced garlic for extra flavor if desired.

Roast in the Oven:
- Roast the asparagus bundles in the preheated oven for about 12-15 minutes or until the asparagus is tender yet still crisp. Cooking time may vary depending on the thickness of the asparagus.

Optional Enhancements:
- If desired, sprinkle lemon zest or grated Parmesan cheese over the roasted asparagus bundles for added freshness and flavor during the last few minutes of roasting.

Serve:
- Remove the bundles from the oven and carefully transfer them to a serving plate. Remove the twine before serving.

Enjoy:

- Serve the Roasted Asparagus Bundles immediately, and enjoy this tasty and visually appealing side dish.

Tips:

- Uniform Size: Try to choose asparagus spears of similar thickness to ensure even roasting.
- Creative Variations: Experiment with different seasonings such as balsamic glaze, crushed red pepper flakes, or toasted almonds for added texture.

Roasted Asparagus Bundles are a wonderful addition to your dinner table, offering a perfect balance of crispiness and tenderness. They're not only delicious but also make for an eye-catching presentation. Enjoy the vibrant flavors of roasted asparagus!

Heart-Shaped Garlic Bread

Ingredients:

- French baguette or Italian bread
- 1/2 cup unsalted butter, softened
- 3-4 cloves garlic, minced
- 2 tablespoons fresh parsley, finely chopped
- Salt, to taste
- Shredded mozzarella cheese (optional)

Instructions:

Preheat Oven:
- Preheat your oven to 375°F (190°C).

Prepare Bread:
- Slice the baguette or Italian bread into 1-inch thick slices.

Cut Heart Shapes:
- Using a heart-shaped cookie cutter or a knife, cut each slice of bread into a heart shape. You can also freehand the heart shape with a knife if you don't have a cookie cutter.

Garlic Butter Mixture:
- In a bowl, mix softened butter, minced garlic, chopped parsley, and a pinch of salt. Adjust the amount of garlic and salt based on your taste preferences.

Spread Garlic Butter:
- Spread the garlic butter mixture generously over each heart-shaped bread slice. Make sure to cover the entire surface.

Optional Cheese Topping:
- If desired, sprinkle shredded mozzarella cheese over the garlic butter for a cheesy variation.

Bake:
- Place the prepared heart-shaped garlic bread on a baking sheet and bake in the preheated oven for about 8-10 minutes or until the edges are golden and the bread is crispy.

Serve Warm:
- Remove from the oven and let the garlic bread cool slightly before serving.

Serve and Enjoy:
- Arrange the heart-shaped garlic bread on a serving platter and serve warm as a charming side to your main dish.

Tips:

- Variations: Experiment with different herbs such as oregano, thyme, or basil in the garlic butter mixture for added flavor.
- Creative Presentation: Arrange the heart-shaped garlic bread on a plate in the shape of a flower or heart cluster for a romantic presentation.

Heart-shaped garlic bread is a fun and lovely addition to a special meal, whether you're celebrating Valentine's Day or simply adding a touch of romance to your dinner. Enjoy the heartwarming flavors!

Parmesan Roasted Brussels Sprouts

Ingredients:

- 1 pound Brussels sprouts, trimmed and halved
- 2 tablespoons olive oil
- Salt and black pepper, to taste
- 1/2 cup grated Parmesan cheese
- 1-2 cloves garlic, minced (optional)
- Lemon wedges, for serving (optional)

Instructions:

Preheat Oven:
- Preheat your oven to 400°F (200°C).

Prepare Brussels Sprouts:
- Trim the ends of the Brussels sprouts and cut them in half. Remove any loose or discolored outer leaves.

Toss with Olive Oil:
- In a large bowl, toss the halved Brussels sprouts with olive oil until they are evenly coated. Add minced garlic if desired.

Season:
- Season the Brussels sprouts with salt and black pepper to taste. Toss again to ensure even seasoning.

Roast in the Oven:
- Spread the Brussels sprouts in a single layer on a baking sheet. Roast in the preheated oven for 20-25 minutes, or until the edges are crispy and golden brown. Stir or shake the pan halfway through cooking for even roasting.

Add Parmesan Cheese:
- In the last 5 minutes of roasting, sprinkle the grated Parmesan cheese over the Brussels sprouts. This allows the cheese to melt and become golden.

Serve:
- Remove the Brussels sprouts from the oven and transfer them to a serving dish. Optionally, squeeze fresh lemon juice over the top before serving for a burst of freshness.

Enjoy:
- Serve the Parmesan Roasted Brussels Sprouts immediately as a flavorful and nutritious side dish.

Tips:

- Browning: For extra crispiness, leave the Brussels sprouts in the oven for a few extra minutes until they are deeply browned and caramelized.
- Variations: Experiment with additional seasonings such as crushed red pepper flakes, balsamic glaze, or a drizzle of honey for a different flavor profile.

This Parmesan Roasted Brussels Sprouts recipe is a simple yet tasty way to enjoy this nutritious vegetable. The combination of roasting and Parmesan cheese adds a delightful depth of flavor. Enjoy as a side dish for your favorite meals!

Desserts:

Chocolate Covered Strawberries

Ingredients:

- Fresh strawberries, washed and dried
- Dark, milk, or white chocolate (chopped or in chocolate chips)
- Optional: White chocolate, for drizzling
- Optional: Chopped nuts, shredded coconut, sprinkles for decoration

Instructions:

Prepare Strawberries:
- Wash and thoroughly dry the strawberries. Make sure they are completely dry to help the chocolate adhere better.

Melt Chocolate:
- Place the chocolate in a heatproof bowl. You can use a microwave or a double boiler for melting. If using a microwave, heat in short intervals, stirring between each, until the chocolate is fully melted and smooth.

Dip Strawberries:
- Hold a strawberry by the stem and dip it into the melted chocolate, covering it about two-thirds of the way. Allow any excess chocolate to drip off.

Optional Decorations:
- If desired, roll the dipped strawberry in chopped nuts, shredded coconut, or sprinkles while the chocolate is still wet for added texture and flavor.

Place on Parchment Paper:
- Place the chocolate-covered strawberries on a parchment paper-lined tray or plate. Ensure they are not touching each other.

Set Chocolate:
- Allow the chocolate-covered strawberries to set at room temperature. You can speed up the process by placing them in the refrigerator for about 15-20 minutes.

Optional Drizzle:
- If using white chocolate for drizzling, melt it similarly to the dark or milk chocolate. Use a fork or a piping bag to drizzle the white chocolate over the set strawberries for an elegant finish.

Serve:

- Once the chocolate is fully set, transfer the chocolate-covered strawberries to a serving plate.

Enjoy:
- Serve and enjoy your homemade chocolate-covered strawberries!

Tips:

- Quality Chocolate: Use high-quality chocolate for the best flavor and texture.
- Variations: Experiment with different types of chocolate, or even add a touch of sea salt for a sweet and salty combination.

Chocolate-covered strawberries are not only delicious but also make for a beautiful and romantic dessert. They are perfect for celebrations or as a sweet gift for someone special. Enjoy!

Red Velvet Cupcakes

Ingredients:

- 1 1/4 cups all-purpose flour
- 1/2 teaspoon baking soda
- 1/2 teaspoon baking powder
- 1/4 teaspoon salt
- 1/2 cup unsalted butter, softened
- 1 cup granulated sugar
- 2 large eggs
- 2 tablespoons unsweetened cocoa powder
- 2 tablespoons red food coloring
- 1 teaspoon vanilla extract
- 1/2 cup buttermilk

Instructions:

Preheat Oven:
- Preheat your oven to 350°F (175°C). Line a muffin tin with cupcake liners.

Combine Dry Ingredients:
- In a medium bowl, whisk together the flour, baking soda, baking powder, and salt.

Cream Butter and Sugar:
- In a large bowl, cream together the softened butter and granulated sugar until light and fluffy.

Add Eggs:
- Add the eggs one at a time, beating well after each addition.

Mix in Cocoa and Food Coloring:
- In a small bowl, mix the cocoa powder and red food coloring to form a paste. Add this paste and vanilla extract to the butter-sugar mixture. Mix until well combined.

Alternate Dry Ingredients and Buttermilk:
- Gradually add the dry ingredients to the wet ingredients in three parts, alternating with the buttermilk. Begin and end with the dry ingredients. Mix until just combined.

Fill Cupcake Liners:
- Divide the batter evenly among the cupcake liners, filling each about 2/3 full.

Bake:

- Bake in the preheated oven for 18-20 minutes or until a toothpick inserted into the center comes out clean.

Cool:
- Allow the cupcakes to cool in the tin for a few minutes, then transfer them to a wire rack to cool completely.

Cream Cheese Frosting:

Ingredients:

- 8 oz (226g) cream cheese, softened
- 1/2 cup (115g) unsalted butter, softened
- 4 cups (480g) powdered sugar
- 1 teaspoon vanilla extract

Instructions:

Beat Cream Cheese and Butter:
- In a large bowl, beat together the softened cream cheese and butter until smooth and creamy.

Add Powdered Sugar:
- Gradually add the powdered sugar, one cup at a time, beating well after each addition.

Add Vanilla Extract:
- Mix in the vanilla extract until well combined.

Frost Cupcakes:
- Once the cupcakes are completely cooled, frost them with the cream cheese frosting using a piping bag or a spatula.

Optional: Decorate:
- Optionally, decorate the cupcakes with sprinkles or grated chocolate.

Enjoy:
- Serve and enjoy these delicious homemade Red Velvet Cupcakes!

These Red Velvet Cupcakes with Cream Cheese Frosting are a classic treat, perfect for any celebration or simply satisfying your sweet tooth. Enjoy!

Molten Lava Cakes

Ingredients:

- 1/2 cup (1 stick) unsalted butter
- 4 ounces semi-sweet or bittersweet chocolate, chopped
- 1 cup powdered sugar
- 2 large eggs
- 2 egg yolks
- 1 teaspoon vanilla extract
- 1/4 cup all-purpose flour
- Pinch of salt
- Optional: Vanilla ice cream or whipped cream for serving

Instructions:

Preheat Oven:
- Preheat your oven to 425°F (220°C). Grease and flour or use cocoa powder to coat four ramekins or oven-safe bowls.

Melt Butter and Chocolate:
- In a microwave-safe bowl or using a double boiler, melt the butter and chopped chocolate together until smooth. Stir well to combine.

Add Powdered Sugar:
- Stir in the powdered sugar until well combined with the chocolate mixture.

Add Eggs and Vanilla:
- Add the eggs and egg yolks one at a time, mixing well after each addition. Stir in the vanilla extract.

Add Flour and Salt:
- Sift in the flour and add a pinch of salt. Gently fold the dry ingredients into the chocolate mixture until just combined. Be careful not to overmix.

Fill Ramekins:
- Divide the batter evenly among the prepared ramekins.

Bake:
- Place the filled ramekins on a baking sheet and bake in the preheated oven for 12-14 minutes. The edges should be set, but the center should still be soft.

Serve Immediately:
- Carefully remove the molten lava cakes from the oven. Let them cool for a minute or two. Run a knife around the edges to loosen, then invert the cakes onto serving plates.

Optional: Serve with Ice Cream or Whipped Cream:
- Serve the molten lava cakes immediately, either as they are or with a scoop of vanilla ice cream or a dollop of whipped cream.

Enjoy:
- Dig in and enjoy the gooey, molten chocolate center of these delicious lava cakes!

Tips:

- Timing is Crucial: Keep a close eye on the baking time. The goal is to have a set edge and a gooey center.
- Ramekin Size: If you use smaller or larger ramekins, adjust the baking time accordingly.

These Molten Lava Cakes are a crowd-pleaser and perfect for a special dessert. The rich, gooey chocolate center is sure to satisfy any chocolate lover's cravings!

Raspberry Chocolate Mousse

Ingredients:

For the Chocolate Mousse:

- 6 ounces (170g) semi-sweet chocolate, chopped
- 2 tablespoons unsalted butter
- 3 large eggs, separated
- 1/4 cup granulated sugar
- 1 teaspoon vanilla extract
- 1 cup heavy cream

For the Raspberry Sauce:

- 1 cup fresh or frozen raspberries
- 2 tablespoons granulated sugar
- 1 tablespoon lemon juice

Optional Garnish:

- Fresh raspberries
- Mint leaves
- Chocolate shavings

Instructions:

Chocolate Mousse:

Melt Chocolate and Butter:
- In a heatproof bowl, melt the chopped chocolate and butter together using a double boiler or in short intervals in the microwave. Stir until smooth and set aside to cool slightly.

Whip Egg Yolks and Sugar:
- In a separate bowl, whisk together the egg yolks and sugar until pale and slightly thickened. Add the vanilla extract and mix well.

Combine with Chocolate Mixture:
- Gradually add the melted chocolate mixture to the egg yolk mixture, stirring continuously to ensure smooth incorporation.

Whip Egg Whites:
- In another clean, dry bowl, whip the egg whites until stiff peaks form.

Fold in Egg Whites:

- Gently fold the whipped egg whites into the chocolate mixture until well combined. Be careful not to deflate the egg whites.

Whip Heavy Cream:
- In a separate bowl, whip the heavy cream until stiff peaks form.

Fold in Whipped Cream:
- Fold the whipped cream into the chocolate mixture until the mousse is light and fluffy.

Chill:
- Divide the chocolate mousse into serving glasses or ramekins. Refrigerate for at least 2 hours or until set.

Raspberry Sauce:

Prepare Raspberry Sauce:
- In a saucepan, combine raspberries, sugar, and lemon juice. Cook over medium heat, stirring occasionally, until the raspberries break down and the sauce thickens slightly.

Strain (Optional):
- If you prefer a smoother sauce, strain the raspberry mixture through a fine mesh sieve to remove seeds. Allow the sauce to cool.

Assemble:
- Once the chocolate mousse is set, spoon a layer of raspberry sauce over each portion.

Garnish:
- Garnish with fresh raspberries, mint leaves, or chocolate shavings if desired.

Serve:
- Serve the Raspberry Chocolate Mousse chilled and enjoy the delightful combination of flavors!

Tips:

- Quality Chocolate: Use good-quality chocolate for a rich and indulgent flavor.
- Make Ahead: This dessert can be prepared a day in advance, making it perfect for entertaining.

Raspberry Chocolate Mousse is a perfect way to end a special meal with a burst of chocolatey and fruity goodness. Enjoy the luxurious and velvety texture of this delightful dessert!

Heart-Shaped Linzer Cookies

Ingredients:

For the Cookies:

- 1 cup unsalted butter, softened
- 1/2 cup granulated sugar
- 1 large egg
- 1 teaspoon vanilla extract
- 2 1/2 cups all-purpose flour
- 1/2 teaspoon baking powder
- 1/4 teaspoon salt
- 1/2 cup ground almonds or almond meal

For the Filling:

- Raspberry or strawberry jam
- Powdered sugar, for dusting

Instructions:

Preheat Oven:
- Preheat your oven to 350°F (180°C). Line baking sheets with parchment paper.

Cream Butter and Sugar:
- In a large bowl, cream together the softened butter and granulated sugar until light and fluffy.

Add Egg and Vanilla:
- Add the egg and vanilla extract to the butter-sugar mixture. Mix until well combined.

Combine Dry Ingredients:
- In a separate bowl, whisk together the flour, baking powder, salt, and ground almonds.

Mix Wet and Dry Ingredients:
- Gradually add the dry ingredients to the wet ingredients, mixing until a soft dough forms.

Chill Dough:
- Divide the dough in half. Wrap each portion in plastic wrap and chill in the refrigerator for at least 1 hour.

Roll Out Dough:
- On a lightly floured surface, roll out one portion of the chilled dough to about 1/4 inch thickness.

Cut Out Shapes:
- Using heart-shaped cookie cutters, cut out an even number of hearts. For half of them, use a smaller heart-shaped cutter to cut out the centers.

Bake:
- Place the cookies on the prepared baking sheets and bake in the preheated oven for 10-12 minutes or until the edges are lightly golden.

Cool:
- Allow the cookies to cool on the baking sheets for a few minutes, then transfer them to a wire rack to cool completely.

Assemble:
- Spread a small amount of raspberry or strawberry jam on the solid heart-shaped cookies. Place a cut-out heart-shaped cookie on top to create a sandwich.

Dust with Powdered Sugar:
- Dust the top of each cookie with powdered sugar.

Serve and Enjoy:
- Serve these delightful Heart-Shaped Linzer Cookies and enjoy the sweet and fruity flavor!

Tips:

- Jam Variation: Feel free to use other types of jams or preserves for a variety of flavors.
- Customize Shapes: Get creative with different shapes and sizes for a unique assortment of cookies.

These Heart-Shaped Linzer Cookies are not only delicious but also make for a beautiful and heartfelt gift or a lovely addition to any celebration. Enjoy the sweet joy these cookies bring!

Drinks:

Raspberry Champagne Cocktail

Ingredients:

- 1 cup fresh raspberries
- 1/4 cup simple syrup (equal parts water and sugar, dissolved)
- 1 bottle of chilled champagne or sparkling wine
- Fresh mint leaves for garnish (optional)

Instructions:

- Prepare Simple Syrup:
  - In a small saucepan, heat equal parts water and sugar over low heat, stirring until the sugar dissolves. Allow the simple syrup to cool.
- Muddle Raspberries:
  - In a bowl or glass, muddle the fresh raspberries to release their juices. You can use the back of a spoon or a muddler for this.
- Add Simple Syrup:
  - Pour the cooled simple syrup over the muddled raspberries and stir to combine.
- Strain Raspberry Mixture (Optional):
  - If you prefer a smoother texture, you can strain the raspberry mixture to remove the seeds. Use a fine mesh sieve or cheesecloth to strain into a bowl or pitcher.
- Prepare Champagne Glasses:
  - Divide the raspberry mixture among champagne glasses, adding about 1-2 tablespoons to each glass.
- Pour Champagne:
  - Top each glass with chilled champagne or sparkling wine. Pour slowly to minimize fizz.
- Garnish:
  - Garnish the Raspberry Champagne Cocktails with fresh mint leaves for a touch of freshness and aroma.
- Serve Immediately:
  - Serve the cocktails immediately while they are bubbly and refreshing.

Tips:

- Frozen Raspberries: If fresh raspberries are not available, you can use frozen raspberries. Allow them to thaw slightly before muddling.
- Chilled Ingredients: Ensure that both the champagne and raspberry mixture are well-chilled for a crisp and refreshing cocktail.

This Raspberry Champagne Cocktail is a beautiful and flavorful drink that adds a festive touch to any celebration. Cheers and enjoy the sparkling goodness!

Strawberry Mint Lemonade

Ingredients:

- 1 cup fresh strawberries, hulled and halved
- 1/2 cup fresh mint leaves
- 1 cup fresh lemon juice (about 4-6 lemons)
- 1 cup granulated sugar (adjust to taste)
- 4 cups cold water
- Ice cubes
- Lemon slices and mint sprigs for garnish (optional)

Instructions:

Prepare Strawberries and Mint:
- Wash and hull the strawberries, then cut them in half. Wash the mint leaves.

Make Strawberry Mint Puree:
- In a blender or food processor, combine the strawberries, mint leaves, and 1/2 cup of water. Blend until you have a smooth puree.

Strain (Optional):
- If you prefer a smoother lemonade, you can strain the strawberry mint puree through a fine mesh sieve to remove the pulp. Press the mixture with the back of a spoon to extract all the liquid.

Prepare Lemon Juice:
- Squeeze fresh lemons to obtain 1 cup of lemon juice.

Make Lemonade Base:
- In a pitcher, combine the strawberry mint puree, fresh lemon juice, granulated sugar, and cold water. Stir well until the sugar is completely dissolved.

Adjust Sweetness:
- Taste the lemonade and adjust the sweetness by adding more sugar if needed. Keep in mind that the sweetness can vary depending on personal preference and the tartness of the strawberries and lemons.

Chill:
- Refrigerate the lemonade for at least 1-2 hours to allow the flavors to meld and the drink to chill.

Serve:
- Fill glasses with ice cubes and pour the Strawberry Mint Lemonade over the ice.

Garnish (Optional):
- Garnish with lemon slices and mint sprigs for a decorative touch.

Enjoy:
- Stir, sip, and enjoy the refreshing Strawberry Mint Lemonade!

Tips:

- Sparkling Variation: Add sparkling water or club soda for a fizzy version of this lemonade.
- Lemon Zest: For an extra burst of lemon flavor, you can add a bit of lemon zest to the strawberry mint puree.

This Strawberry Mint Lemonade is a perfect blend of sweet, tangy, and herbal flavors.

It's a wonderful way to quench your thirst on a hot day or add a burst of summery

goodness to any occasion. Cheers!

Chocolate Martini

Ingredients:

- 2 oz (60 ml) chocolate liqueur (such as Godiva or Crème de Cacao)
- 1 oz (30 ml) vanilla vodka
- 1 oz (30 ml) heavy cream or chocolate milk
- Ice cubes
- Chocolate syrup for rimming the glass (optional)
- Chocolate shavings or cocoa powder for garnish (optional)

Instructions:

Prepare Glass (Optional):
- If desired, rim a martini glass with chocolate syrup. Dip the rim of the glass into a shallow dish of chocolate syrup to coat it evenly.

Fill Shaker with Ice:
- Fill a cocktail shaker with ice cubes.

Add Ingredients:
- Pour the chocolate liqueur, vanilla vodka, and heavy cream (or chocolate milk) into the shaker.

Shake Well:
- Secure the lid on the shaker and shake the mixture vigorously for about 15-20 seconds. This helps chill the ingredients and create a frothy texture.

Strain into Glass:
- Strain the contents of the shaker into the prepared martini glass.

Garnish (Optional):
- Garnish the Chocolate Martini with chocolate shavings or a sprinkle of cocoa powder on top.

Serve:
- Serve the Chocolate Martini immediately while it's cold and frothy.

Tips:

- Variation with Chocolate Milk: If you prefer a creamier texture, you can use chocolate milk instead of heavy cream. Adjust the quantity to achieve your desired taste and consistency.
- Chocolate Liqueur Choices: Experiment with different chocolate liqueurs to find your preferred level of sweetness and chocolate flavor.

This Chocolate Martini is a luxurious and sweet cocktail, making it a perfect after-dinner drink or a delightful treat for special occasions. Enjoy the rich and velvety taste of chocolate in every sip!

Breakfast/Brunch:

Heart-Shaped Pancakes

Ingredients:

- 1 cup all-purpose flour
- 2 tablespoons sugar
- 1 teaspoon baking powder
- 1/2 teaspoon baking soda
- 1/4 teaspoon salt
- 3/4 cup buttermilk
- 1/4 cup milk
- 1 large egg
- 2 tablespoons unsalted butter, melted
- 1 teaspoon vanilla extract
- Cooking spray or additional butter for greasing the pan

Instructions:

Preheat Griddle or Pan:
- Preheat a griddle or non-stick skillet over medium heat.

Prepare Dry Ingredients:
- In a large bowl, whisk together the flour, sugar, baking powder, baking soda, and salt.

Prepare Wet Ingredients:
- In another bowl, whisk together the buttermilk, milk, egg, melted butter, and vanilla extract.

Combine Wet and Dry Ingredients:
- Pour the wet ingredients into the dry ingredients and gently stir until just combined. It's okay if there are a few lumps.

Shape Heart Pancakes:
- Lightly grease the griddle or skillet with cooking spray or butter. Pour or ladle the pancake batter onto the griddle to form heart shapes. You can freehand the heart shape or use a heart-shaped pancake mold.

Cook Until Bubbles Form:
- Cook the pancakes until bubbles form on the surface, and the edges start to look set.

Flip and Cook Other Side:

- Carefully flip the pancakes with a spatula and cook the other side until golden brown.

Serve Warm:
- Remove the heart-shaped pancakes from the griddle and place them on a serving plate.

Optional Toppings:
- Serve the pancakes warm with your favorite toppings such as maple syrup, fresh berries, whipped cream, or a dusting of powdered sugar.

Enjoy:
- Enjoy these adorable Heart-Shaped Pancakes with your loved ones for a special and heartwarming breakfast or brunch!

Tips:

- Consistent Heart Shapes: Use a heart-shaped pancake mold or cookie cutter for consistent and well-defined heart shapes.
- Keep Warm: If making a large batch, you can keep the pancakes warm in a low-temperature oven until ready to serve.

These heart-shaped pancakes are not only delicious but also a lovely way to show appreciation to those you share breakfast with. Enjoy the warmth and joy these pancakes bring to your morning!

Eggs Benedict with Heart-Shaped Toast

Ingredients:

- 1 cup all-purpose flour
- 2 tablespoons sugar
- 1 teaspoon baking powder
- 1/2 teaspoon baking soda
- 1/4 teaspoon salt
- 3/4 cup buttermilk
- 1/4 cup milk
- 1 large egg
- 2 tablespoons unsalted butter, melted
- 1 teaspoon vanilla extract
- Cooking spray or additional butter for greasing the pan

Instructions:

Preheat Griddle or Pan:
- Preheat a griddle or non-stick skillet over medium heat.

Prepare Dry Ingredients:
- In a large bowl, whisk together the flour, sugar, baking powder, baking soda, and salt.

Prepare Wet Ingredients:
- In another bowl, whisk together the buttermilk, milk, egg, melted butter, and vanilla extract.

Combine Wet and Dry Ingredients:
- Pour the wet ingredients into the dry ingredients and gently stir until just combined. It's okay if there are a few lumps.

Shape Heart Pancakes:
- Lightly grease the griddle or skillet with cooking spray or butter. Pour or ladle the pancake batter onto the griddle to form heart shapes. You can freehand the heart shape or use a heart-shaped pancake mold.

Cook Until Bubbles Form:
- Cook the pancakes until bubbles form on the surface, and the edges start to look set.

Flip and Cook Other Side:
- Carefully flip the pancakes with a spatula and cook the other side until golden brown.

Serve Warm:

- Remove the heart-shaped pancakes from the griddle and place them on a serving plate.

Optional Toppings:
- Serve the pancakes warm with your favorite toppings such as maple syrup, fresh berries, whipped cream, or a dusting of powdered sugar.

Enjoy:
- Enjoy these adorable Heart-Shaped Pancakes with your loved ones for a special and heartwarming breakfast or brunch!

Tips:

- Consistent Heart Shapes: Use a heart-shaped pancake mold or cookie cutter for consistent and well-defined heart shapes.
- Keep Warm: If making a large batch, you can keep the pancakes warm in a low-temperature oven until ready to serve.

These heart-shaped pancakes are not only delicious but also a lovely way to show appreciation to those you share breakfast with. Enjoy the warmth and joy these pancakes bring to your morning!

Red Velvet Waffles

Ingredients:

- 2 cups all-purpose flour
- 1/4 cup unsweetened cocoa powder
- 1 tablespoon sugar
- 1 tablespoon baking powder
- 1/2 teaspoon baking soda
- 1/2 teaspoon salt
- 2 large eggs
- 1 3/4 cups buttermilk
- 1/2 cup unsalted butter, melted
- 1 tablespoon red food coloring
- 1 teaspoon vanilla extract
- Cooking spray or additional butter for greasing the waffle iron

Instructions:

Preheat Waffle Iron:
- Preheat your waffle iron according to the manufacturer's instructions.

Combine Dry Ingredients:
- In a large bowl, whisk together the flour, cocoa powder, sugar, baking powder, baking soda, and salt.

Whisk Wet Ingredients:
- In another bowl, whisk together the eggs, buttermilk, melted butter, red food coloring, and vanilla extract.

Combine Wet and Dry Ingredients:
- Pour the wet ingredients into the dry ingredients and stir until just combined. The batter may be slightly lumpy.

Grease Waffle Iron:
- Lightly grease the preheated waffle iron with cooking spray or butter.

Cook Waffles:
- Pour the red velvet waffle batter onto the center of the waffle iron, spreading it slightly to cover the waffle grid.

Cook According to Waffle Iron Instructions:
- Close the waffle iron and cook according to the manufacturer's instructions, typically for about 3-5 minutes or until the waffles are golden brown and cooked through.

Repeat:

- Repeat the process with the remaining batter.

Serve Warm:
- Serve the Red Velvet Waffles warm with your favorite toppings, such as cream cheese glaze, whipped cream, fresh berries, or a dusting of powdered sugar.

Enjoy:
- Enjoy these decadent Red Velvet Waffles as a delightful treat for breakfast or brunch!

Cream Cheese Glaze (Optional):

For an extra touch, you can prepare a simple cream cheese glaze to drizzle over the waffles:

- 4 oz cream cheese, softened
- 1/2 cup powdered sugar
- 1/2 teaspoon vanilla extract
- 2-3 tablespoons milk
  In a bowl, beat together the softened cream cheese, powdered sugar, and vanilla extract until smooth.
  Gradually add milk, one tablespoon at a time, until the glaze reaches your desired consistency.
  Drizzle the cream cheese glaze over the warm Red Velvet Waffles before serving.

Tips:

- Adjust the amount of red food coloring to achieve the desired level of redness in your waffles.
- Be cautious not to overfill the waffle iron to prevent batter overflow.

These Red Velvet Waffles are a delightful and festive addition to your breakfast or brunch repertoire. Enjoy the rich and vibrant flavors!

Extras:

Heart-Shaped Fruit Salad

Ingredients:

- Assorted fruits (choose a variety of colors for visual appeal):
    - Strawberries
    - Watermelon
    - Pineapple
    - Kiwi
    - Grapes
    - Mango
    - Blueberries
    - Raspberries

Instructions:

Prepare Fruits:
- Wash and peel the fruits as needed. Remove stems, seeds, and cores. Cut larger fruits into bite-sized pieces.

Slice Strawberries:
- Slice strawberries into thin rounds. These will be used to create the outer edge of the heart shape.

Cut Watermelon:
- Cut watermelon into thick slices. Use a heart-shaped cookie cutter to cut out heart shapes from the watermelon slices.

Cut Remaining Fruits:
- Cut the remaining fruits into bite-sized pieces. For example, dice pineapples, cube mangoes, halve or quarter grapes, and slice kiwi.

Arrange Heart Shape:
- On a large serving platter or individual plates, arrange the sliced strawberries in the shape of a heart. Place the heart-shaped watermelon cutouts along the outer edge to complete the heart shape.

Fill Heart with Assorted Fruits:
- Fill the center of the heart shape with the assorted fruit pieces. Be creative with the arrangement and mix colors for an eye-catching display.

Garnish (Optional):

- Garnish the fruit salad with a few whole berries or mint leaves for an extra touch of freshness.

Serve Chilled:
- Refrigerate the fruit salad for a short time to chill before serving. However, keep in mind that some fruits, like watermelon, are best served fresh.

Enjoy:
- Serve the Heart-Shaped Fruit Salad as a healthy and visually appealing dish for breakfast, brunch, or any special occasion.

Tips:

- Use a variety of fruits for a colorful and diverse presentation.
- Get creative with your arrangement; you can even use toothpicks to skewer some fruit pieces for added height.

This Heart-Shaped Fruit Salad not only looks beautiful but also provides a tasty and nutritious option for a refreshing start to the day or as a delightful addition to a festive spread. Enjoy the vibrant flavors of the season!

Love Potion No. 9 Smoothie

Ingredients:

- 1 cup frozen mixed berries (strawberries, blueberries, raspberries)
- 1/2 cup frozen cherries
- 1 ripe banana
- 1/2 cup plain or vanilla yogurt
- 1 cup pomegranate juice
- 1-2 tablespoons honey or agave syrup (optional, depending on sweetness preference)
- Ice cubes (optional, for a colder and thicker smoothie)
- Fresh berries for garnish (optional)

Instructions:

Prepare Ingredients:
- If you haven't already, freeze the mixed berries and cherries. Make sure the banana is ripe and peeled.

Blend Ingredients:
- In a blender, combine the frozen mixed berries, frozen cherries, ripe banana, yogurt, and pomegranate juice.

Add Sweetener (Optional):
- If you prefer a sweeter smoothie, add honey or agave syrup to taste. Start with a small amount and adjust according to your sweetness preference.

Blend Until Smooth:
- Blend all the ingredients until smooth and well combined. If the smoothie is too thick, you can add more pomegranate juice or a splash of water.

Adjust Consistency:
- If you want a colder and thicker smoothie, you can add a handful of ice cubes and blend again until smooth.

Serve:
- Pour the Love Potion No. 9 Smoothie into glasses.

Garnish (Optional):
- Garnish with fresh berries on top for a decorative touch.

Enjoy:
- Sip and enjoy this fruity and refreshing Love Potion No. 9 Smoothie!

Tips:

- Feel free to get creative and customize the smoothie with other fruits or juices that you love.
- If using fresh berries instead of frozen, you can add more ice cubes to achieve the desired thickness.

This Love Potion No. 9 Smoothie is not only delicious but also a delightful way to add a touch of magic to your day. Whether you enjoy it on your own or share it with someone special, it's sure to bring a smile!

Cocktails:

Pomegranate Martini

Ingredients:

- 2 oz (60 ml) pomegranate juice
- 2 oz (60 ml) vodka
- 1/2 oz (15 ml) triple sec or orange liqueur
- 1/2 oz (15 ml) fresh lime juice
- 1/2 oz (15 ml) simple syrup (adjust to taste)
- Ice cubes
- Pomegranate seeds or lime twist for garnish (optional)

Instructions:

Prepare Martini Glass:
- Place a martini glass in the freezer for a few minutes to chill.

Combine Ingredients:
- In a cocktail shaker, add pomegranate juice, vodka, triple sec, fresh lime juice, and simple syrup.

Add Ice:
- Fill the shaker with ice cubes.

Shake Well:
- Secure the lid on the shaker and shake the mixture vigorously for about 15-20 seconds. This helps chill the ingredients and create a frothy texture.

Strain into Glass:
- Strain the contents of the shaker into the chilled martini glass.

Garnish (Optional):
- Garnish with pomegranate seeds or a twist of lime for an extra touch of flair.

Serve:
- Serve the Pomegranate Martini immediately while it's cold and refreshing.

Tips:

- Pomegranate Juice: If possible, use fresh pomegranate juice for the best flavor. You can also use store-bought pomegranate juice.
- Simple Syrup: Adjust the amount of simple syrup based on your sweetness preference. Start with a smaller amount and add more if needed.

This Pomegranate Martini is a perfect cocktail for any occasion, with its vibrant color and delightful blend of flavors. Sip and enjoy the sweet and tart notes of this delicious martini!

Rose Sangria

Ingredients:

- 1 bottle (750 ml) of chilled rosé wine
- 1/4 cup brandy
- 1/4 cup orange liqueur (such as triple sec)
- 2 tablespoons sugar (adjust to taste)
- 1 cup sliced strawberries
- 1 cup sliced peaches or nectarines
- 1 cup raspberries
- 1 cup seedless grapes (red or green)
- 1 medium orange, thinly sliced
- 1-2 cups chilled club soda or sparkling water (adjust to taste)
- Ice cubes
- Fresh mint leaves for garnish (optional)

Instructions:

Prepare Fruits:
- Wash and prepare the fruits as needed. Slice strawberries, peaches or nectarines, and the orange. If using grapes, you can keep them whole or slice them in half.

Combine Wine and Spirits:
- In a large pitcher, combine the chilled rosé wine, brandy, orange liqueur, and sugar. Stir until the sugar is dissolved.

Add Sliced Fruits:
- Add the sliced strawberries, peaches or nectarines, raspberries, grapes, and orange slices to the pitcher. Stir gently to combine.

Chill:
- Place the pitcher in the refrigerator and let the sangria chill for at least 2-4 hours, allowing the flavors to meld.

Add Club Soda:
- Just before serving, add chilled club soda or sparkling water to the sangria. Start with 1 cup and adjust to your desired level of fizziness.

Stir and Serve:
- Give the sangria a gentle stir to mix in the club soda. Taste and adjust the sweetness if needed.

Add Ice:
- Fill glasses with ice cubes.

Pour and Garnish:
- Pour the Rose Sangria into the glasses over the ice. Garnish with fresh mint leaves if desired.

Enjoy:
- Sip and enjoy the refreshing and fruity goodness of Rose Sangria!

Tips:

- Experiment with Fruits: Feel free to customize the fruits based on what's in season or your personal preferences.
- Chill Time: Allowing the sangria to chill for a few hours or overnight enhances the flavors.

This Rose Sangria is perfect for warm weather gatherings, brunch, or any occasion where you want to share a flavorful and vibrant drink with friends and family. Cheers!

Champagne Jello Shots

Ingredients:

- 1 cup champagne or sparkling wine
- 1/2 cup orange juice (or any fruit juice of your choice)
- 2 tablespoons sugar (adjust to taste)
- 3 envelopes (21 grams) unflavored gelatin powder
- Fresh fruit slices (optional, for garnish)

Instructions:

Prepare Mixture:
- In a saucepan, combine champagne, orange juice, and sugar. Sprinkle the unflavored gelatin over the liquid and let it sit for a few minutes to bloom.

Heat Mixture:
- Heat the mixture over low heat, stirring continuously until the gelatin and sugar completely dissolve. Do not boil; just heat until the mixture is smooth.

Remove from Heat:
- Remove the saucepan from heat and let the mixture cool for a few minutes.

Pour into Molds:
- Pour the mixture into your chosen molds. You can use silicone molds, small cups, or even citrus halves (like orange or lemon halves, hollowed out).

Chill:
- Place the molds in the refrigerator and let the Champagne Jello Shots chill until fully set. This typically takes at least 2-4 hours.

Garnish (Optional):
- If desired, garnish the set Jello shots with fresh fruit slices just before serving.

Serve:
- Pop the Champagne Jello Shots out of the molds or serve them in the cups.

Enjoy Responsibly:
- Serve and enjoy these bubbly and fun Champagne Jello Shots responsibly!

Tips:

- Champagne Choice: Use a champagne or sparkling wine that you enjoy drinking, as the flavor will come through in the Jello shots.
- Garnish Ideas: Garnish with fresh berries, citrus zest, or edible flowers for an extra touch of elegance.
- Layered Shots: For a visually stunning effect, you can create layers by letting one layer set partially before adding the next layer.

Champagne Jello Shots are a festive and adult-friendly treat that can add a touch of celebration to any gathering. Please remember to consume them responsibly and be mindful of your guests. Cheers!

Romantic Dinners for Two:

Baked Salmon with Lemon-Dill sauce

Ingredients:

For the Baked Salmon:

- 4 salmon fillets
- Salt and pepper, to taste
- 2 tablespoons olive oil
- 2 tablespoons fresh lemon juice
- 2 cloves garlic, minced
- 1 teaspoon dried dill (or 1 tablespoon fresh dill, chopped)
- Lemon slices, for garnish (optional)

For the Lemon-Dill Sauce:

- 1/2 cup plain Greek yogurt
- 2 tablespoons mayonnaise
- 1 tablespoon fresh lemon juice
- 1 tablespoon fresh dill, chopped
- Salt and pepper, to taste

Instructions:

Baked Salmon:

> Preheat Oven:
> - Preheat your oven to 375°F (190°C).
>
> Prepare Salmon:
> - Pat the salmon fillets dry with a paper towel. Season both sides with salt and pepper.
>
> Make Marinade:
> - In a small bowl, whisk together the olive oil, fresh lemon juice, minced garlic, and dried dill.
>
> Marinate Salmon:
> - Place the salmon fillets in a baking dish. Pour the marinade over the salmon, ensuring it's evenly coated. Let it marinate for about 15 minutes.
>
> Bake Salmon:

- Bake the salmon in the preheated oven for 15-20 minutes or until the salmon flakes easily with a fork. Cooking time may vary depending on the thickness of the fillets.

Garnish (Optional):
- Garnish the baked salmon with fresh lemon slices.

Lemon-Dill Sauce:

Prepare Sauce:
- In a small bowl, whisk together the Greek yogurt, mayonnaise, fresh lemon juice, and chopped dill. Season with salt and pepper to taste.

Serve:
- Serve the Baked Salmon with a drizzle of Lemon-Dill Sauce on top or on the side.

Garnish (Optional):
- Garnish with additional fresh dill for a burst of flavor and a touch of freshness.

Tips:

- Freshness Matters: If possible, use fresh dill for both the marinade and the sauce. It adds a bright and vibrant flavor.
- Salmon Thickness: Adjust the baking time based on the thickness of your salmon fillets. Thicker fillets may require a few extra minutes.

This Baked Salmon with Lemon-Dill Sauce is a perfect dish for a healthy and flavorful meal. The combination of the lemon-dill marinade and sauce enhances the natural taste of the salmon. Enjoy this dish with your favorite side dishes or a fresh salad!

Shrimp Scampi

Ingredients:

- 1 pound large shrimp, peeled and deveined
- Salt and black pepper, to taste
- 8 oz linguine or spaghetti
- 3 tablespoons unsalted butter
- 3 tablespoons olive oil
- 4 cloves garlic, minced
- 1/2 teaspoon red pepper flakes (optional, for a bit of heat)
- 1/2 cup dry white wine
- 1/4 cup fresh lemon juice
- Zest of one lemon
- 1/4 cup chopped fresh parsley
- Grated Parmesan cheese, for serving

Instructions:

Prepare Shrimp:
- Pat the shrimp dry with paper towels. Season with salt and black pepper.

Cook Pasta:
- Cook the linguine or spaghetti according to the package instructions until al dente. Reserve about 1/2 cup of pasta cooking water. Drain and set aside.

Sauté Shrimp:
- In a large skillet, heat 2 tablespoons of butter and 2 tablespoons of olive oil over medium-high heat. Add the shrimp and cook for 1-2 minutes per side until they turn pink. Remove the shrimp from the skillet and set aside.

Make Sauce:
- In the same skillet, add the remaining 1 tablespoon of butter and 1 tablespoon of olive oil. Add minced garlic and red pepper flakes (if using). Sauté for about 1 minute until the garlic becomes fragrant.

Deglaze with Wine:
- Pour in the white wine, scraping the bottom of the skillet to deglaze and incorporate the flavorful bits. Allow the wine to simmer for 1-2 minutes.

Add Lemon and Shrimp:
- Stir in the fresh lemon juice and lemon zest. Return the cooked shrimp to the skillet and toss to coat in the sauce. Cook for an additional 2-3 minutes.

Combine Pasta:
- Add the cooked and drained pasta to the skillet. Toss everything together, coating the pasta in the flavorful sauce. If needed, add a bit of the reserved pasta cooking water to loosen the sauce.

Finish with Parsley:
- Stir in chopped fresh parsley. Taste and adjust seasoning with salt and black pepper.

Serve:
- Serve the Shrimp Scampi hot, garnished with additional parsley and grated Parmesan cheese.

Tips:

- Variations: You can customize Shrimp Scampi by adding cherry tomatoes, spinach, or other favorite ingredients.
- Wine Substitute: If you prefer not to use wine, you can replace it with chicken broth.

This Shrimp Scampi is a quick and elegant dish that's perfect for a weeknight dinner or a special occasion. The combination of garlic, lemon, and shrimp creates a delightful flavor that pairs well with pasta. Enjoy!

Couples Cooking Class Pizza

Homemade Pizza Dough:

Ingredients:

- 2 1/4 teaspoons (1 packet) active dry yeast
- 1 teaspoon sugar
- 3/4 cup warm water (110°F/43°C)
- 2 cups all-purpose flour
- 1 teaspoon salt
- 1 tablespoon olive oil

Instructions:

Activate Yeast:
- In a bowl, combine the warm water, sugar, and yeast. Let it sit for about 5-10 minutes until the mixture becomes frothy.

Prepare Dough:
- In a large mixing bowl, combine the flour and salt. Make a well in the center and add the activated yeast mixture and olive oil. Mix until a dough forms.

Knead:
- Transfer the dough to a floured surface and knead for about 5-7 minutes until it becomes smooth and elastic.

First Rise:
- Place the dough in a lightly oiled bowl, cover with a clean kitchen towel, and let it rise in a warm place for 1-2 hours or until it doubles in size.

Preheat Oven:
- Preheat your oven to the highest temperature it can go (usually around 475°F/245°C).

Roll Out Dough:
- Punch down the risen dough and roll it out on a floured surface to your desired thickness.

Pizza Toppings:

Classic Margherita Pizza:

- Tomato sauce
- Fresh mozzarella cheese, sliced

- Fresh basil leaves
- Olive oil
- Salt and pepper

BBQ Chicken Pizza:

- Barbecue sauce
- Cooked and shredded chicken
- Red onion, thinly sliced
- Mozzarella cheese
- Cilantro, chopped

Mediterranean Pizza:

- Pesto sauce or olive tapenade
- Cherry tomatoes, halved
- Kalamata olives, sliced
- Feta cheese, crumbled
- Fresh oregano, chopped

Veggie Delight Pizza:

- Tomato sauce or garlic-infused olive oil
- Bell peppers, thinly sliced
- Red onion, thinly sliced
- Mushrooms, sliced
- Spinach leaves
- Mozzarella cheese

Pizza Making Instructions:

Assemble Pizzas:
- Spread your chosen sauce over the rolled-out pizza dough and add your favorite toppings.

Bake:
- Transfer the pizzas to a preheated oven and bake for about 10-15 minutes, or until the crust is golden and the cheese is melted and bubbly.

Serve:
- Slice the pizzas and serve hot. Don't forget to enjoy your creations together!

Tips:

- Get Creative: Encourage each other to get creative with toppings and shapes. You can even make heart-shaped pizzas for a romantic touch.
- Enjoy the Process: The joy of making pizzas together is just as important as eating them. Have fun, laugh, and savor the experience.

A homemade pizza night can turn into a memorable and enjoyable couples' activity. So roll up your sleeves, get your favorite toppings ready, and create delicious pizzas together!

Sweets and Treats:

Valentine's Day Truffles

Ingredients:

For the Truffles:

- 8 oz (about 225g) good quality dark chocolate, finely chopped
- 1/2 cup (120 ml) heavy cream
- 2 tablespoons unsalted butter, softened
- 1 teaspoon vanilla extract

For Coatings (Optional):

- Cocoa powder
- Finely chopped nuts (e.g., pistachios, almonds, or hazelnuts)
- Shredded coconut
- Powdered sugar
- Sprinkles
- Edible gold dust or colored sugar (for a festive touch)

Instructions:

Prepare Chocolate:
- Place the finely chopped dark chocolate in a heatproof bowl.

Heat Cream:
- In a small saucepan, heat the heavy cream over medium heat until it just begins to boil. Pour the hot cream over the chopped chocolate. Let it sit for a minute to melt the chocolate.

Mix and Add Butter:
- Gently stir the chocolate and cream until smooth and well combined. Add the softened butter and vanilla extract, stirring until the mixture is glossy.

Chill:
- Cover the bowl with plastic wrap and chill the chocolate mixture in the refrigerator for at least 2 hours or until it becomes firm enough to handle.

Shape Truffles:
- Once chilled, use a spoon or a melon baller to scoop out portions of the chocolate mixture. Roll each portion into a small ball, placing them on a parchment-lined tray.

Coat Truffles:

- Roll each truffle in your choice of coating. You can have a variety of coatings for a diverse selection.

Chill Again:
- Place the coated truffles back in the refrigerator for about 30 minutes to firm up.

Serve and Gift:
- Once the truffles are set, arrange them in a decorative box or on a plate. These make a lovely homemade Valentine's Day gift.

Tips:

- Flavor Variations: You can customize the truffles by adding flavorings such as a hint of orange zest, a splash of flavored liqueur, or a pinch of your favorite spice.
- Storage: Store the truffles in an airtight container in the refrigerator. Bring them to room temperature before serving.

Creating homemade Valentine's Day truffles is a sweet and thoughtful way to express your love. Enjoy sharing these delightful treats with your special someone!

Heart-Shaped Red Velvet Whoopie Pies

Ingredients:

For the Red Velvet Whoopie Pies:

- 2 cups all-purpose flour
- 2 tablespoons cocoa powder
- 1/2 teaspoon baking powder
- 1/4 teaspoon baking soda
- 1/4 teaspoon salt
- 1/2 cup unsalted butter, softened
- 1 cup granulated sugar
- 1 large egg
- 1 teaspoon vanilla extract
- 1 tablespoon red food coloring
- 1 cup buttermilk

For the Cream Cheese Filling:

- 8 oz cream cheese, softened
- 1/2 cup unsalted butter, softened
- 2 cups powdered sugar
- 1 teaspoon vanilla extract

Instructions:

Red Velvet Whoopie Pies:

Preheat Oven:
- Preheat your oven to 350°F (175°C). Line baking sheets with parchment paper.

Prepare Dry Ingredients:
- In a medium bowl, sift together flour, cocoa powder, baking powder, baking soda, and salt. Set aside.

Cream Butter and Sugar:
- In a large bowl, cream together the softened butter and granulated sugar until light and fluffy.

Add Egg and Flavorings:
- Beat in the egg and vanilla extract. Add the red food coloring and mix until well combined.

Alternate Dry Ingredients and Buttermilk:

- Gradually add the dry ingredients to the wet ingredients, alternating with buttermilk. Begin and end with the dry ingredients, mixing just until combined.

Form Heart Shapes:
- Using a heart-shaped cookie cutter or a template, drop spoonfuls of batter onto the prepared baking sheets, shaping them into heart shapes. Leave enough space between each heart.

Bake:
- Bake in the preheated oven for 10-12 minutes or until the edges are set. Allow them to cool on the baking sheets for a few minutes before transferring to a wire rack to cool completely.

Cream Cheese Filling:

Beat Cream Cheese and Butter:
- In a large bowl, beat the softened cream cheese and butter until smooth and creamy.

Add Sugar and Vanilla:
- Gradually add the powdered sugar and vanilla extract, continuing to beat until well combined.

Assemble Whoopie Pies:
- Once the red velvet hearts are completely cooled, spread or pipe the cream cheese filling onto the flat side of half of the hearts. Top with the remaining hearts to create heart-shaped whoopie pies.

Serve:
- Serve and enjoy these delightful heart-shaped red velvet whoopie pies with your loved ones!

Tips:

- Consistency of Batter: The batter should be thick enough to hold its shape when forming the heart shapes. If it's too thin, add a little more flour; if it's too thick, add a splash of buttermilk.
- Cream Cheese Filling: Adjust the sweetness of the cream cheese filling according to your taste by adding more or less powdered sugar.

These heart-shaped red velvet whoopie pies are not only visually appealing but also incredibly delicious. Share them with your special someone or make them as a sweet surprise for Valentine's Day!

Cherry Chocolate Cheesecake

Ingredients:

For the Chocolate Crust:

- 1 1/2 cups chocolate cookie crumbs (graham cracker crumbs or chocolate wafer crumbs)
- 1/4 cup unsalted butter, melted

For the Cheesecake Filling:

- 24 oz (about 680g) cream cheese, softened
- 1 cup granulated sugar
- 3 large eggs
- 1 cup sour cream
- 1 teaspoon vanilla extract
- 1/2 cup all-purpose flour

For the Cherry Topping:

- 2 cups fresh or frozen cherries, pitted and halved
- 1/2 cup granulated sugar
- 1 tablespoon cornstarch
- 1 tablespoon lemon juice

Optional Chocolate Ganache Drizzle:

- 4 oz semi-sweet chocolate, finely chopped
- 1/2 cup heavy cream

Instructions:

Chocolate Crust:

Preheat Oven:
- Preheat your oven to 325°F (163°C). Grease a 9-inch (23 cm) springform pan.

Make Crust:
- In a bowl, combine the chocolate cookie crumbs and melted butter. Press the mixture into the bottom of the prepared springform pan to create the crust.

Bake Crust:
- Bake the crust in the preheated oven for about 10 minutes. Remove from the oven and let it cool while preparing the cheesecake filling.

Cheesecake Filling:

Prepare Filling:
- In a large mixing bowl, beat the softened cream cheese until smooth. Add sugar and beat until well combined.

Add Eggs:
- Add eggs one at a time, beating well after each addition.

Incorporate Sour Cream and Flour:
- Mix in the sour cream and vanilla extract. Gradually add the flour and mix until just combined. Be careful not to overmix.

Pour into Crust:
- Pour the cheesecake filling over the cooled chocolate crust.

Bake Cheesecake:
- Bake in the preheated oven for about 50-60 minutes or until the edges are set, and the center is slightly jiggly.

Cool and Refrigerate:
- Allow the cheesecake to cool in the oven with the door ajar for about an hour, then refrigerate for at least 4 hours or overnight.

Cherry Topping:

Prepare Cherries:
- In a saucepan, combine cherries, sugar, cornstarch, and lemon juice. Cook over medium heat, stirring frequently, until the mixture thickens and the cherries are soft.

Cool:
- Let the cherry topping cool completely before spreading it over the chilled cheesecake.

Chocolate Ganache Drizzle (Optional):

Make Ganache:
- In a heatproof bowl, place chopped chocolate. In a small saucepan, heat the heavy cream until it just begins to simmer. Pour the hot cream over the chocolate and let it sit for a minute. Stir until smooth.

Drizzle Over Cheesecake:
- Drizzle the chocolate ganache over the chilled cheesecake and cherry topping.

Chill Again:
- Place the cheesecake back in the refrigerator to allow the ganache to set.

Serve:
- Once fully set, carefully remove the cheesecake from the springform pan, slice, and serve.

Tips:

- Fresh vs. Frozen Cherries: You can use fresh or frozen cherries for the topping, depending on what's available.
- Ganache Consistency: Adjust the thickness of the chocolate ganache by varying the chocolate-to-cream ratio.

This Cherry Chocolate Cheesecake is sure to be a delightful and indulgent treat, perfect for special occasions or any time you're craving a combination of chocolate and cherry goodness!

Cute and Playful:

Love Bug Cupcakes

Ingredients:

For the Cupcakes:

- 1 box of your favorite chocolate cupcake mix (and ingredients needed as per the box instructions)
- Red or pink food coloring (optional)

For the Frosting:

- 1 cup unsalted butter, softened
- 4 cups powdered sugar
- 1/4 cup cocoa powder
- 1/4 cup milk or cream
- 1 teaspoon vanilla extract

For Decorating:

- Red or pink decorating gel or icing
- Candy eyes
- Red heart-shaped candies or sprinkles
- Chocolate chips or chocolate candies (for the love bug's antennae)

Instructions:

Cupcakes:

    Prepare Cupcake Batter:
- Preheat your oven according to the cupcake mix instructions. Prepare the cupcake batter as directed on the box.

    Add Food Coloring (Optional):
- If you want a deeper red or pink color, add a few drops of food coloring to the batter and mix well.

    Bake Cupcakes:
- Fill cupcake liners with the batter and bake according to the box instructions. Allow the cupcakes to cool completely before frosting.

Frosting:

Make Chocolate Frosting:
- In a large bowl, beat the softened butter until creamy. Add powdered sugar and cocoa powder gradually, alternating with milk or cream. Add vanilla extract and beat until smooth and fluffy.

Frost Cupcakes:
- Once the cupcakes are completely cooled, frost them with the chocolate frosting using a piping bag or a knife.

Decorating Love Bugs:

Draw Hearts:
- Use red or pink decorating gel or icing to draw a heart shape on the top of each cupcake. This will be the love bug's body.

Add Eyes:
- Place two candy eyes on each cupcake, positioning them near the top of the heart shape.

Create Antennae:
- Insert two chocolate chips or chocolate candies into the frosting at the top of each cupcake to create the love bug's antennae.

Give Wings:
- If you have heart-shaped candies or sprinkles, you can use them to create wings for your love bugs. Place one on each side of the heart shape.

Optional Details:
- Use additional decorating gel or icing to add details such as a smiling mouth or additional decorations.

Serve and Enjoy:
- Once decorated, your Love Bug Cupcakes are ready to be served and enjoyed!

Tips:

- Get Creative: Feel free to customize the love bugs with different expressions or accessories.
- Make it a Family Activity: Decorating cupcakes can be a fun and creative activity for kids and adults alike.

These Love Bug Cupcakes are sure to bring joy and smiles to your celebration. Enjoy the process of making and sharing these adorable treats with your loved ones!

Heart-Shaped Rice Krispie Treats

Ingredients:

- 6 cups Rice Krispies cereal
- 10 oz (about 4 cups) mini marshmallows
- 3 tablespoons unsalted butter
- Red or pink food coloring (optional)
- Cooking spray or additional butter for greasing

Instructions:

Prepare Baking Pan:
- Grease a 9x13-inch baking pan with cooking spray or butter. You can also use a heart-shaped cookie cutter if you have one.

Melt Marshmallows and Butter:
- In a large saucepan, melt the butter over low heat. Add the mini marshmallows and stir continuously until completely melted. If you want colored treats, add a few drops of food coloring and mix until well combined.

Add Rice Krispies:
- Remove the saucepan from heat and gently fold in the Rice Krispies cereal until evenly coated with the marshmallow mixture.

Press into Pan:
- Transfer the mixture to the greased baking pan and press it down evenly with a spatula or your hands. If you're using a cookie cutter, press the mixture into the pan first and then use the cutter to create heart shapes.

Cool and Cut:
- Allow the Rice Krispie treats to cool and set for at least 30 minutes. Once they are set, use a heart-shaped cookie cutter to cut out individual treats. If you don't have a cookie cutter, you can cut them into squares and then use a knife to shape them into hearts.

Serve and Enjoy:
- Your heart-shaped Rice Krispie treats are ready to be served and enjoyed!

Tips:

- Add Sprinkles: For an extra festive touch, add heart-shaped sprinkles or colored sugar on top before the treats set.

- Use Cookie Cutters: If you don't have a heart-shaped cookie cutter, you can mold the treats into hearts using your hands or shape them into other fun shapes.

These heart-shaped Rice Krispie treats are a delightful and easy-to-make treat that's perfect for sharing with friends, family, or a special someone. Enjoy spreading the love with these tasty treats!

Chocolate Covered Pretzel Rods

Ingredients:

- Pretzel rods
- 8 to 12 ounces of chocolate (dark, milk, or white chocolate)
- Assorted toppings for decoration (sprinkles, crushed nuts, coconut flakes, etc.)

Instructions:

Prepare Toppings:
- If you're using toppings like sprinkles or crushed nuts, have them ready in separate bowls.

Melt Chocolate:
- Break the chocolate into small pieces and place it in a heatproof bowl. Melt the chocolate using a microwave or a double boiler. If using a microwave, heat in short intervals, stirring in between until smooth.

Dip Pretzel Rods:
- Dip each pretzel rod into the melted chocolate, coating it evenly. Use a spoon or spatula to help spread the chocolate if needed.

Remove Excess Chocolate:
- Allow the excess chocolate to drip off the pretzel rod. You can gently tap the rod against the edge of the bowl to help with this.

Decorate with Toppings:
- While the chocolate is still wet, roll the coated pretzel rod in your chosen toppings. Alternatively, you can sprinkle the toppings over the chocolate.

Set on Parchment Paper:
- Place the chocolate-covered pretzel rods on a parchment paper-lined tray to set. Ensure they are not touching each other.

Allow to Set:
- Let the chocolate set and harden at room temperature. You can also place the tray in the refrigerator for quicker setting.

Optional Drizzle:
- If desired, melt a different type of chocolate (white or dark) and drizzle it over the set pretzel rods for an extra decorative touch.

Serve and Enjoy:
- Once the chocolate is fully set, your chocolate-covered pretzel rods are ready to be served and enjoyed!

Tips:

- Get Creative: Experiment with different types of chocolate and toppings to create a variety of flavors and textures.
- Gift Idea: Tie a ribbon around a bundle of chocolate-covered pretzel rods for a thoughtful and delicious homemade gift.

These chocolate-covered pretzel rods make for a delightful treat for parties, celebrations, or just a sweet snack. The combination of crunchy pretzels and smooth chocolate is always a crowd-pleaser!

Special Breakfast in Bed:

Heart-Shaped Breakfast Burritos

Ingredients:

- 4 large eggs
- Salt and pepper, to taste
- 1 tablespoon butter or cooking oil
- 4 large flour tortillas
- 1 cup cooked and seasoned breakfast sausage or bacon
- 1 cup shredded cheese (cheddar, Monterey Jack, or your favorite)
- Salsa or pico de gallo, for serving
- Avocado slices, for garnish (optional)
- Fresh cilantro or green onions, chopped, for garnish (optional)

Instructions:

Cook Scrambled Eggs:
- In a bowl, whisk the eggs and season with salt and pepper. Heat butter or cooking oil in a skillet over medium heat. Pour in the whisked eggs and scramble until cooked to your liking. Set aside.

Prepare Heart Shapes:
- Lay out the flour tortillas on a clean surface. Use a heart-shaped cookie cutter or a knife to cut heart shapes out of each tortilla. Reserve the excess pieces for later.

Assemble Burritos:
- Place a portion of the cooked scrambled eggs, breakfast sausage or bacon, and shredded cheese onto the center of each heart-shaped tortilla.

Fold and Seal:
- Carefully fold the sides of the tortilla inwards to create the heart shape, ensuring the filling is enclosed. Use a toothpick if needed to secure the pointed end of the heart.

Cook Burritos:
- Heat a skillet over medium heat. Place the heart-shaped burritos seam side down on the skillet and cook until the tortillas are golden brown and crispy on each side.

Serve:

- Remove the toothpick if used. Serve the heart-shaped breakfast burritos warm with salsa or pico de gallo. Garnish with avocado slices, fresh cilantro, or green onions if desired.

Tips:

- Customize Fillings: Feel free to customize the fillings based on your preferences. You can add sautéed vegetables, black beans, or other favorite breakfast ingredients.
- Make-Ahead: Prepare the scrambled eggs and filling ahead of time for a quicker assembly in the morning.

These heart-shaped breakfast burritos are not only adorable but also a delightful way to start your day with a touch of love. Enjoy this creative and tasty breakfast treat!

Berry Parfait

Ingredients:

- 2 cups mixed berries (strawberries, blueberries, raspberries, blackberries)
- 2 cups Greek yogurt (vanilla or plain)
- 1/2 cup granola
- 2 tablespoons honey or maple syrup (optional, for drizzling)
- Mint leaves for garnish (optional)

Instructions:

Prepare Berries:
- Wash and gently pat dry the mixed berries. If using strawberries, hull and slice them.

Layer Yogurt:
- Begin by spooning a layer of Greek yogurt into the bottom of serving glasses or bowls.

Add Berries:
- Place a portion of the mixed berries on top of the yogurt layer. Ensure an even distribution of berries.

Sprinkle Granola:
- Sprinkle a layer of granola over the berries. The granola adds a delightful crunch to the parfait.

Repeat Layers:
- Repeat the layers by adding more yogurt, followed by berries and granola until you reach the top of the serving glass or bowl.

Drizzle Honey (Optional):
- If you like a touch of sweetness, drizzle honey or maple syrup over the top layer of the parfait.

Garnish (Optional):
- Garnish the parfait with a few additional fresh berries on top and mint leaves for a pop of color and freshness.

Serve Immediately:
- Serve the Berry Parfait immediately to enjoy the crisp texture of the granola and the freshness of the berries.

Tips:

- Customize: Feel free to customize the parfait with your favorite fruits, flavored yogurt, or different types of granola.
- Make-Ahead: You can prepare the individual components in advance and assemble the parfait just before serving to maintain the freshness.

This Berry Parfait is not only visually appealing but also a nutritious and delicious way to enjoy the goodness of fresh berries. It's perfect for a light dessert, a refreshing breakfast, or a wholesome snack. Enjoy the burst of flavors in every layer!

Heart-Shaped Avocado Toast

Ingredients:

- 2 slices of your favorite bread (whole grain, sourdough, or multigrain)
- 1 ripe avocado
- Salt and pepper, to taste
- Red pepper flakes (optional, for a bit of heat)
- Lemon juice (optional, to prevent avocado from browning)
- Cherry tomatoes, sliced (for garnish)
- Fresh herbs (such as cilantro or chives), chopped, for garnish

Instructions:

Toast the Bread:
- Toast the slices of bread to your desired level of crispiness.

Prepare Avocado:
- Cut the ripe avocado in half, remove the pit, and scoop the avocado flesh into a bowl. Mash the avocado with a fork until smooth.

Shape the Hearts:
- Using a heart-shaped cookie cutter or a knife, cut heart shapes out of the mashed avocado.

Season Avocado:
- Season the mashed avocado with salt, pepper, and red pepper flakes (if using). Add a splash of lemon juice to prevent browning and for extra flavor.

Spread on Toast:
- Spread the seasoned mashed avocado onto the toasted bread slices, shaping it into a heart.

Garnish:
- Garnish the heart-shaped avocado toast with sliced cherry tomatoes and chopped fresh herbs.

Serve:
- Serve the heart-shaped avocado toast immediately for a lovely and nutritious breakfast.

Tips:

- Customize Toppings: Experiment with additional toppings like poached eggs, feta cheese, or microgreens to add extra flavor and texture.

- Personalize Shapes: If you don't have a heart-shaped cookie cutter, you can try shaping the avocado into other fun shapes or simply spread it onto the toast without shaping.

This heart-shaped avocado toast is not only visually appealing but also a delicious and wholesome breakfast option. It's a perfect way to show some love to yourself or someone special. Enjoy the delightful combination of creamy avocado and crispy toast!

Intimate Dinners:

Steak and Shrimp Surf and Turf

Ingredients:

For the Steak:

- 2 beef tenderloin or ribeye steaks (6-8 oz each)
- Salt and black pepper, to taste
- 2 tablespoons olive oil
- 2 cloves garlic, minced
- 2 sprigs fresh rosemary or thyme (optional)

For the Shrimp:

- 12 large shrimp, peeled and deveined
- 2 tablespoons unsalted butter
- 2 cloves garlic, minced
- 1 tablespoon fresh lemon juice
- 1 tablespoon chopped fresh parsley
- Salt and black pepper, to taste

For Serving:

- Mashed potatoes or roasted vegetables (optional)

Instructions:

Cook the Steak:

    Preheat Oven:
- Preheat your oven to 400°F (200°C).

    Season Steak:
- Pat the steaks dry with paper towels. Season both sides with salt and black pepper.

    Sear the Steak:
- Heat olive oil in an oven-safe skillet over high heat. Sear the steaks for 2-3 minutes on each side until a golden crust forms.

    Add Flavors:

- Add minced garlic and fresh rosemary or thyme (if using) to the skillet. Baste the steaks with the infused oil.

Finish in the Oven:
- Transfer the skillet to the preheated oven and roast for 5-7 minutes for medium-rare, or longer according to your preference.

Rest the Steak:
- Remove the skillet from the oven and let the steaks rest for a few minutes before serving.

Cook the Shrimp:

Prepare Shrimp:
- In a separate skillet, melt butter over medium heat. Add minced garlic and sauté for a minute until fragrant.

Cook Shrimp:
- Add the peeled and deveined shrimp to the skillet. Cook for 2-3 minutes on each side until they turn pink and opaque.

Finish with Flavor:
- Squeeze fresh lemon juice over the shrimp, sprinkle with chopped parsley, and season with salt and black pepper.

Serve:

Plate the Steak and Shrimp:
- Place the cooked steak on a plate, and arrange the shrimp on top.

Optional Side:
- Serve the Steak and Shrimp Surf and Turf with your choice of sides, such as mashed potatoes or roasted vegetables.

Garnish:
- Garnish with additional fresh herbs or a drizzle of the pan juices.

Enjoy the Intimate Dinner:
- Serve immediately and enjoy this delightful and decadent surf and turf dinner.

Tips:

- Temperature Guide for Steak:
    - Rare: 125°F (52°C)
    - Medium Rare: 135°F (57°C)
    - Medium: 145°F (63°C)
    - Medium Well: 150°F (66°C)

- Well Done: 160°F (71°C)
- Personalize Flavors: Feel free to add your favorite herbs, spices, or a splash of wine to the pan for extra flavor.

This Steak and Shrimp Surf and Turf is sure to impress and create a memorable dining experience for your intimate dinner. Enjoy the combination of succulent steak and perfectly cooked shrimp!

Pasta in Pink Vodka Sauce

Ingredients:

- 8 oz (about 225g) penne or your favorite pasta
- 2 tablespoons olive oil
- 1 small onion, finely chopped
- 2 cloves garlic, minced
- 1/4 teaspoon red pepper flakes (optional, for heat)
- 1 can (28 oz) crushed tomatoes
- 1/4 cup vodka
- 1/2 cup heavy cream
- Salt and black pepper, to taste
- 1/4 cup grated Parmesan cheese
- Fresh basil or parsley, chopped, for garnish

Instructions:

Cook Pasta:
- Cook the pasta according to the package instructions in a large pot of salted boiling water until al dente. Drain and set aside.

Prepare Sauce:
- In a large skillet, heat olive oil over medium heat. Add chopped onions and cook until softened, about 2-3 minutes. Add minced garlic and red pepper flakes (if using) and sauté for an additional 1 minute.

Add Crushed Tomatoes:
- Pour in the crushed tomatoes and stir well. Allow the mixture to simmer for about 10-15 minutes, stirring occasionally.

Incorporate Vodka:
- Pour in the vodka and let the sauce simmer for an additional 5-7 minutes to cook off the alcohol. Stir occasionally.

Add Cream:
- Lower the heat, pour in the heavy cream, and stir until the sauce becomes creamy. Season with salt and black pepper to taste.

Combine Pasta and Sauce:
- Add the cooked pasta to the sauce, tossing to coat the pasta evenly.

Finish and Garnish:
- Stir in grated Parmesan cheese and continue to cook until the cheese is melted and the sauce has thickened. Adjust seasoning if needed.

Serve:

- Plate the Pasta in Pink Vodka Sauce and garnish with chopped fresh basil or parsley.

Enjoy:
- Serve immediately and enjoy your creamy and flavorful pasta in pink vodka sauce!

Tips:

- Customize Ingredients: You can add cooked shrimp, chicken, or vegetables to the pasta for additional protein or a vegetarian version.
- Adjust Consistency: If the sauce becomes too thick, you can add a bit of pasta cooking water to reach your desired consistency.

This Pasta in Pink Vodka Sauce is a delicious and elegant dish perfect for a special meal. The vodka adds a unique depth of flavor to the sauce, and the creaminess makes it a comforting and satisfying choice. Enjoy your delightful pasta creation!

Vegetarian Heart-Stuffed Bell Peppers

Ingredients:

- 4 large bell peppers (red, yellow, or orange)
- 1 cup quinoa, cooked
- 1 can (15 oz) black beans, drained and rinsed
- 1 cup corn kernels (fresh or frozen)
- 1 cup cherry tomatoes, diced
- 1 cup shredded cheese (cheddar or Mexican blend)
- 1 teaspoon cumin powder
- 1 teaspoon chili powder
- 1/2 teaspoon garlic powder
- Salt and pepper, to taste
- 1/4 cup fresh cilantro, chopped
- Salsa, guacamole, or sour cream for serving (optional)

Instructions:

Preheat Oven:
- Preheat your oven to 375°F (190°C).

Prepare Bell Peppers:
- Cut the tops off the bell peppers and remove the seeds and membranes. Cut a V-shaped notch at the top to create a heart shape. If needed, slice a thin piece from the bottom to help the peppers stand upright.

Cook Quinoa:
- Cook quinoa according to package instructions. Set aside.

Prepare Filling:
- In a large bowl, combine cooked quinoa, black beans, corn, cherry tomatoes, shredded cheese, cumin powder, chili powder, garlic powder, salt, and pepper. Mix well.

Stuff Bell Peppers:
- Stuff each bell pepper with the quinoa mixture, pressing down gently to pack the filling. Top each pepper with additional cheese if desired.

Bake:
- Place the stuffed bell peppers in a baking dish. Bake in the preheated oven for 25-30 minutes or until the peppers are tender.

Garnish:
- Remove from the oven and sprinkle chopped cilantro over the stuffed peppers.

Serve:
- Serve the Vegetarian Heart-Stuffed Bell Peppers with salsa, guacamole, or sour cream if desired.

Tips:

- Variations: Customize the filling with your favorite vegetables, beans, or grains.
- Protein Boost: Add tofu, tempeh, or plant-based ground meat to increase the protein content.

These Vegetarian Heart-Stuffed Bell Peppers are a delightful and nutritious choice for a romantic dinner or any special occasion. The heart-shaped presentation adds a touch of love to the meal. Enjoy this flavorful and colorful dish!